I Need More Coffee: Brewing Your Financial Success

Kingsley David

Disclaimer

I Need More Coffee: Brewing Your Financial Success

Kingsley David © 2023– All Rights Reserved

No part of this book may be reproduced, stored, or transmitted in any form or by any means, including mechanical or electronic, without prior written permission from the author.

While the author has made every effort to ensure that the ideas, statistics, and the information presented in this book are accurate to the best of his/her abilities, any implications direct, derived, or perceived, should only be used at the reader's discretion.

The author cannot be held responsible for any personal or commercial damage arising from communication, application, or misinterpretation of the information presented herein.

All Rights Reserved.

3

TABLE OF CONTENTS

INTRODUCTION

Welcome to this unique journey through the world of personal finance, where the aroma of coffee serves as our guiding light. Just as you savor the nuances of your favorite brew, we're about to dive into the complex flavors of financial wisdom.

Do you ever find yourself craving that steaming cup of coffee in the morning, unable to start your day without it? Or perhaps you're the type who can't resist the allure of a cozy coffee shop, with each visit bringing an opportunity to try a new blend or espresso concoction.

If you find yourself nodding along, then welcome to the club of caffeine lovers. The aroma of freshly brewed coffee is our daily motivation, our trusted companion in times of need, and often, our financial kryptonite.

In the guiding light of your favorite brew, let's embark on a journey that is both practical and, dare I say, addictive. We will explore the intricate world of personal finance using coffee, one of life's most beloved elixirs. You might wonder how coffee and finance can possibly be related. Well, dear reader, grab your favorite mug, pour yourself a cup, and let's dive in.

Imagine your daily coffee run as a microcosm of your overall financial life. When making financial decisions, it's important to give them the same level of scrutiny as you would when buying coffee.

Both coffee choices and financial choices involve decision-making. Each time you step into a café or reach for your coffee maker, you're making choices about what kind of coffee to enjoy, how much to spend, and whether it's a necessary expense. When it comes to personal finance, you must decide how to allocate your money based on your priorities and indulgences.

So, if you're ready to embark on this unique and caffeine-fueled adventure through the world of personal finance, turn the page and let's get started. Just as that first sip of coffee invigorates your senses, the knowledge you'll gain here will empower you to take control of your financial future. It's time to blend the love of coffee with the wisdom of finance, creating a brew of success that's rich, satisfying, and truly enjoyable.

CHAPTER 1: THE COFFEE BUDGET

Ah, that first sip of morning coffee – it's like a caffeinated hug for your soul. But have you ever stopped to think about the financial journey each cup represents? Imagine this: you're standing in line at your favorite café, and the barista greets you with a warm smile. It's a routine you're familiar with, and you know exactly what you want – a venti, half-caf, extra shot, soy milk, no foam latte with a dash of caramel. The barista nods, and you're charged accordingly.

Our journey into the world of personal finance begins by showing us the importance of crafting a financial blend, much like a barista creates the perfect cup of coffee. We'll also see how a budget serves as the recipe for financial success and how you can balance your income and expenses while savoring the essence of savings.

YOUR FINANCIAL BLEND RECIPE

Think of your budget as the barista's recipe for that delightful cup of coffee. It starts with a clear plan, specifying the right ingredients and proportions. Your financial blend, just like your coffee, can be customized to your unique taste and preferences. A good budgeting skill is a valuable tool that can help you achieve your financial goals and lead a more fulfilling life.

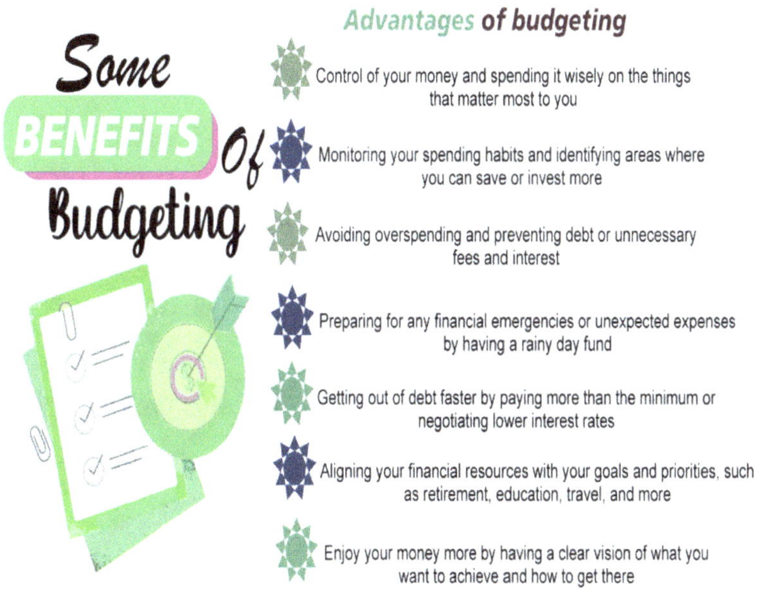

Creating an ideal budget is a skill that you can learn, just like a barista knows how to make the perfect cup of coffee. You enjoy your coffee every day, similarly, you can benefit from your budget every month.

THE ART OF BALANCING INCOME AND EXPENSES

As you take that first sip, think of it as your daily financial decision. Balancing income and expenses is an art that requires attention to detail. As you are particular about your coffee order, you should be meticulous about your spending choices. Each of your expenses, whether a daily cup of coffee, or a larger purchase, demands consideration.

Creating a budget is an essential financial planning tool that helps you manage your money, track your expenses, and work toward your financial goals.

Step-By-Step Guide to Creating a Budget

STEP 1: Your Financial Goals
- Identify your short-term and long-term financial goals. These may include saving for a vacation, paying off debt, or building an emergency fund.

STEP 2: Gather Financial Information
- Collect all your financial documents, including bank statements, pay stubs, bills, and any other financial records. This will give you a clear picture of your income and expenses.

STEP 3: Calculate Your Total Income
- List all sources of income, including your salary, rental income, freelance work, and any other regular income. Calculate your total monthly income.

STEP 4: List Your Monthly Expenses
- Categorize your expenses into fixed and variable categories. Common expense categories include housing, utilities, transportation, groceries, and entertainment, insurance, and debt payments. Track your expenses for a few months to get an accurate picture of your spending habits.

STEP 5: Calculate Your Total Expenses
- Add up all your monthly expenses. This will give you an overview of how much you're spending each month.

STEP 6: Determine Disposable Income
- Subtract your fixed expenses from your total income. The result is your disposable income, which is the money you have left after covering your basic expenses.

STEP 7: Create Your Budget
- Allocate your disposable income to various expense categories based on your priorities and financial goals. Ensure that you allocate enough for savings and debt repayment. Use budgeting software or spreadsheet tools to organize and track your budget.

STEP 8: Stick to Your Budget
- Adhere to the spending limits you've set for each category in your budget. Continuously track your expenses and compare them to your budget to ensure you stay on track.

STEP 9: Adjust Your Budget
- Life circumstances and financial goals may change, so be prepared to adjust your budget accordingly. If you find that you're consistently overspending in certain categories, consider reallocating funds from less critical areas.

STEP 10: Monitor Your Progress
- Regularly review your budget and assess your progress toward your financial goals. Celebrate your achievements and make necessary adjustments to stay on course.

STEP 11: Build Emergency Fund
- As your financial situation improves, prioritize building an emergency fund and saving for long-term goals, such as retirement or major purchases.

STEP 12: Seek Professional Advice
- If you have complex financial goals or face significant challenges, consider consulting a financial advisor for expert guidance.

A skilled barista knows the precise amount of beans and water needed for the perfect brew, and similarly, you need to measure your income and expenses to create a balanced financial plan.

THE 50-30-20 BUDGETING RULE

Managing your finances and allocating your income is crucial, but it can be overwhelming. The 50-30-20 budgeting rule is a popular and straightforward guideline that can help you with this task. It suggests dividing your monthly income into three main categories.

50% for Needs

 First, allocate 50% of your income for essential expenses or needs, such as rent or mortgage payments, utilities, groceries, transportation, insurance premiums, and other necessary bills. This category ensures you have a stable foundation and can meet your basic obligations.

30% for Wants

Second, reserve 30% of your income for discretionary spending, often referred to as wants. This category encompasses non-essential expenses like dining out, entertainment, travel, shopping for non-essential items, and other lifestyle choices. It allows you to enjoy your income and have some flexibility for personal preferences and leisure activities.

20% for Savings and Debt Repayment

Third, dedicate the remaining 20% of your income to savings and debt reduction. This portion can be further divided between savings for future goals (such as an emergency fund, retirement, or a down payment on a home) and paying down high-interest debts, like credit card balances. Building savings and reducing debt helps secure your financial future. It's important to remember that individual circumstances can vary, and you may need to adjust these percentages based on your unique financial goals and situation.

The 50-30-20 budgeting rule provides a straightforward framework to ensure you balance your financial priorities. It serves as a starting point for budgeting and can be customized to fit your needs and aspirations. Creating and maintaining a budget is an ongoing process that requires discipline and commitment, but it's a powerful tool for gaining control of your finances and achieving your financial objectives.

Let me explain a simple analogy to help you understand your financial situation better. Imagine two coffee cups, one for your income and the other for your expenses. The coffee beans represent the money flowing in and out of your financial situation.

Income Cup

The "Income" cup represents all the money you earn, including your salary, rental income, freelance work, or any other sources of income. Each coffee bean you put into this cup signifies a certain amount of money you earn.

Expenses Cup

The "Expenses" cup represents your monthly or periodic expenses, such as rent/mortgage, groceries, utilities, transportation, entertainment, and so on. Each coffee bean you put into this cup signifies an expense you have to pay.

The Take Home Lessons

* The key to financial stability is to ensure that your "Income" coffee cup always has more coffee beans (money) than your "Expenses" coffee cup.

* Always monitor your income and expenses. If you find that your "Expenses" cup is filling up faster than your "Income" cup, it's time to make some adjustments.

* You can reduce your expenses by cutting unnecessary costs or finding more cost effective ways to spend your money.

* Conversely, you can increase your income by seeking better job opportunities, investing wisely, or exploring additional sources of income like a side business or investments.

The goal is to keep your "Income" cup consistently fuller than your "Expenses" cup to maintain a healthy financial balance. The key to financial success is not just about balancing these cups for a single month but creating a sustainable and long-term financial plan that allows you to save and invest for the future while covering your current expenses.

CHAPTER 2: THE COFFEE SAVINGS ACCOUNT

This chapter will discuss the concept of a "coffee savings account" and how regular savings can help you reach your financial goals. Just as you carefully select your coffee beans and measure the right  amount of water, you need to be equally meticulous when it comes to saving and investing your money.

Coffee is more than just caffeine; it's an experience. It's the anticipation as you wait for the coffee to brew, the aroma that fills the room, and the warmth of the cup in your hands. Similarly, financial planning is about more than just numbers; it's about creating a plan that brings your dreams to life.

Imagine your financial dreams as a complex coffee blend, each element contributing to its unique flavor. Savings play a crucial role in achieving these dreams, just as quality coffee beans are the foundation of a great brew. Remember, just as the right beans and brew time result in a perfect cup of coffee, making mindful financial choices will lead to financial success.

THE POWER OF REGULAR SAVINGS

Think of your savings as the coffee beans of your financial blend and your daily coffee habit as a metaphor for consistent saving. They form the foundation of your financial journey. The key factor in both coffee brewing and financial planning is consistency.

Regular contributions to your coffee savings account can lead to financial stability and growth. Just as a coffee drip method yields a consistent flavor, consistent actions can brew up a significant financial pot.

Whether you save for emergencies, future goals, or retirement, the power of consistent savings should not be underestimated. It's a simple yet effective way to grow your financial resources and achieve your financial objectives.

Let's see how small daily savings can add up significantly over time. This illustration shows that a modest daily savings habit can lead to a substantial accumulation of funds.

Small Daily Savings Can Add Up Significantly Over Time

STEP 1

Initial Savings

Start with an empty coffee cup, and label it "Initial Savings."

Pour a handful of coffee beans into the "Initial Savings" cup. These beans represent your initial savings, let's say $100.

STEP 2

Daily Savings

Take another coffee cup, and label it "Daily Savings."

Every day, add a few coffee beans into the "Daily Savings" cup to represent the money you save. For example, save $2 per day.

Step 3

Weekly Accumulation

After a week, you'll have saved $2 x 7 days = $14.

Pour the $14 from the "Daily Savings" cup into the "Initial Savings" cup to represent the savings from the first week. Now, you have $100 (initial savings) + $14 (first week's savings) = $114 in the "Initial Savings" cup.

Step 4

Monthly Accumulation

After a month (30 days), you'll have saved $2 x 30 days = $60.

Pour the $60 from the "Daily Savings" cup into the "Initial Savings" cup to represent the savings from the first month. Now, you have $100 (initial savings) + $60 (first month's savings) = $160 in the "Initial Savings" cup.

Step 5

Yearly Accumulation

After a year (365 days), you'll have saved $2 x 365 days = $730.

Pour the $730 coffee beans from the "Daily Savings" cup into the "Initial Savings" cup to represent the savings from the first year. Now, you have $100 (initial savings) + $730 (first year's savings) = $830 in the "Initial Savings" cup.

Step 6

Reflect on the Accumulation

By consistently saving just $2 per day, you've managed to accumulate $730 in one year.

THE FUTURE TASTES BRIGHT

As you sip your coffee, remember that every dollar saved and invested is a step closer to your financial dreams. Just as a coffee connoisseur savors each brew, you can savor the financial security and opportunities that disciplined saving and investing bring.

The Coffee Savings Jar

Ever thought of creating a coffee savings jar? It's a fun way to visualize your financial goals. For every cup of coffee you skip making at home, you put the equivalent amount into your savings jar. It's a tasty way to watch your savings grow!

CHAPTER 3: THE LATTE FACTOR AND SMALL EXPENSES

Have you ever heard of the "latte factor"? It's a concept that suggests small daily expenses can add up to a significant amount over time. Just as coffee aficionados appreciate the nuances of a perfectly brewed cup, we're about to discover the subtleties of managing small daily expenses that can impact your financial future.

Think of your daily cup of coffee as a small, recurring expense - the daily latte, the occasional pastry, the convenience store snack, and all those little indulgences that bring comfort and joy to our lives. But here's the twist: what if we told you that these seemingly small expenses could be the key to unlocking substantial savings?

MAKING THE ESPRESSO SHOT COUNT

Let's compare the daily cost of coffee to other small daily expenses like a snack or a streaming subscription. This will help to highlight the significant impact of these seemingly trivial choices on your finances over time. Let's break down the comparison.

Coffee

Cost

Let's say you spend $4 on a coffee every workday.

Monthly Cost: 20 workdays x $4 = $80

Annual Cost: $80 x 12 months = $960

Impact

While a daily coffee may seem like a minor expense, it can add up to nearly $1,000 annually. This money could be saved or invested to help you reach your financial goals.

Streaming Subscription

Cost

A popular streaming service subscription costs $15 per month.

Annual Cost: $15 x 12 months = $180

Impact

Enjoying streaming content is a common expense today. However, it's essential to consider if you're getting enough value from your subscriptions to justify the cost. Cutting out one or reassessing multiple subscriptions can lead to substantial savings.

<table>
<tr><td colspan="2" align="center">Snack</td></tr>
<tr>
<td>Cost

Suppose you buy a $2 snack each workday.

Monthly Cost: 20 workdays x $2 = $40

Annual Cost: $40 x 12 months = $480</td>
<td>Impact

Regularly indulging in daily snacks can cost you almost $500 annually. Cutting down on unnecessary snacking can free up funds for more meaningful expenses.</td>
</tr>
</table>

Emphasis on Small Daily Choices

It's important to remember that small daily expenses can add up to significant annual costs. The choices you make every day can either help you achieve your financial goals or hinder your progress. By cutting back on daily coffee, and snacks, or reassessing subscriptions, you can free up some funds for savings, investments, or paying down debt.

Creating a budget and tracking your daily expenses can help you become more aware of where your money is going and make informed decisions about your spending. Over time, these small daily choices can have a profound impact on your financial well-being. Redirecting even a portion of these daily expenses towards savings or investments can help you build wealth and achieve your financial aspirations.

BREWING WEALTH THROUGH MINDFUL SPENDING

Like a master barista crafting a perfect cup of coffee, it's important you are mindful of your spending habits. Instead of spending your money without much thought, think of each expense as an opportunity to make a choice - to spend or to save. Mindful spending is like selecting premium coffee beans, ensuring that your financial blend is of the highest quality.

The Process of Making Mindful Spending Choices

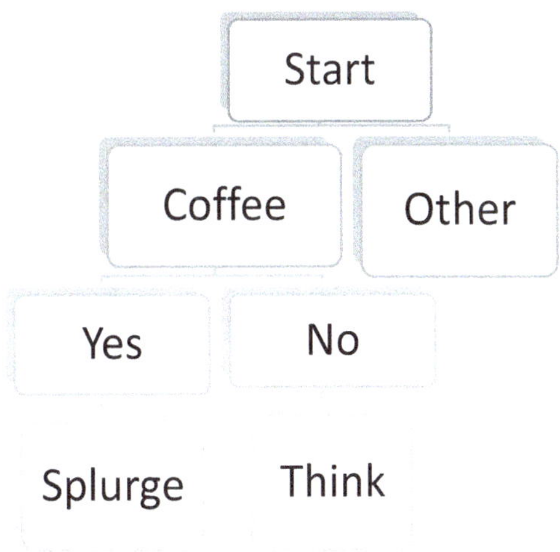

Explanation of the Decision Tree

- **Start**

  This is the starting point when you're faced with a spending decision.

- **Coffee or Other**

  The first choice is whether the expense in question is related to coffee (e.g., buying coffee from a café) or something else (e.g., another discretionary purchase).

- **Yes or No**

  Depending on your choice, you decide whether you want to proceed with the expense (Yes) or reconsider it (No).

- **Splurge**

  If you choose "Yes" for coffee, you're opting to splurge and indulge in the coffee expense.

- **Think**

If you choose "No" for coffee or "Other," it's time to pause and think. Consider the following questions:

- Is this expense a necessity or a luxury?

- Can I afford it within my budget without sacrificing other financial goals?

- Will this expense bring me long-term satisfaction and value?

- Are there more cost-effective alternatives or ways to reduce this expense?

- Is there a better use for this money, such as saving or investing for the future?

The decision tree encourages you to pause and reflect on your spending choices, especially for discretionary expenses like buying coffee or other non-essential items. It helps you make more mindful spending decisions by considering your financial goals and priorities before making a purchase.

Mindful Spending to Increased Savings Journey

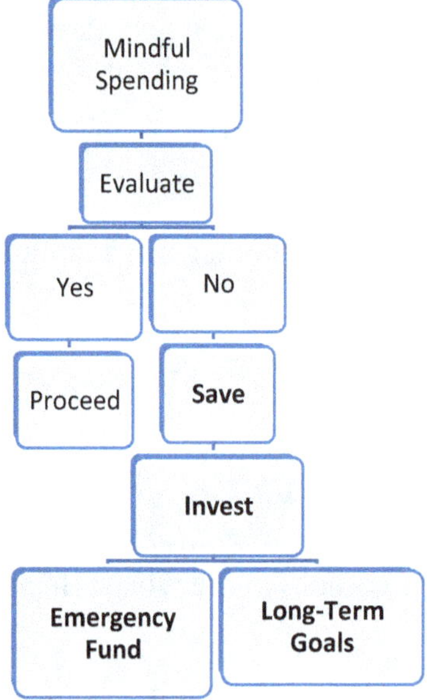

Explanation of the Journey

❖ **Mindful Spending**

This is where you begin, with the intention of spending money thoughtfully and purposefully.

❖ **Evaluate**

The first step in mindful spending is to evaluate your expenses. Ask yourself questions like:

- Is this purchase necessary?

- Does it align with my values and goals?

- Can I find a more cost-effective option?

- Will it provide long-term satisfaction or is it a short-term impulse?

❖ **Cut**

If, after evaluating, you determine that an expense isn't essential or aligned with your goals, consider cutting it from your budget.

❖ **Proceed**

If the expense passes your evaluation and you decide it's worth it, you proceed with the spending.

❖ **Save**

For every expense you evaluate and decide not to proceed with, allocate the money you would have spent to savings.

❖ **Invest**

As your savings grow, you can choose to invest them for potential long-term growth. Investments can include stocks, bonds, real estate, and other assets.

❖ **Emergency Fund**

Part of your savings can be dedicated to building an emergency fund, which acts as a financial safety net for unexpected expenses.

❖ **Long-Term Goals**

Another portion of your savings can go toward achieving your long-term financial goals, such as retirement, buying a home, or funding your children's education.

The journey from mindful spending to increased savings involves a systematic approach to evaluating expenses, making conscious choices, and directing the money saved toward financial security and future aspirations. This process empowers you to take control of your finances, reduce unnecessary spending, and work toward a more secure financial future.

TRIMMING THE FOAM: CUTTING UNNECESSARY EXPENSES

Think about the foam on your cappuccino – it's delightful, but do you really need that extra froth? Similarly, in your finances, there are likely expenses that are delightful but not entirely necessary. Identifying and trimming these unnecessary expenses can free up money for more meaningful financial goals.

As you continue to enjoy your daily coffee, remember that each small expense you cut or redirect is a step towards financial freedom and security. Just as a coffee lover savors the intricate flavors of a well-brewed cup, you can savor the satisfaction of controlling your finances and shaping your financial future.

CHAPTER 4: COFFEE AND DEBT

We have talked about the importance of financial discipline and how trimming unnecessary expenses can help us achieve our financial goals. However, there is another aspect of personal finance that can be challenging - debt. Just like we sometimes consume too much caffeine, we can find ourselves trapped in a cycle of financial debt.

Think of debt as the bitter espresso shot in your financial journey. Using a credit card for everyday purchases might feel convenient and satisfying, but over time, the charges can add up. Similarly, debt can become a heavy burden that's hard to get rid of.

From Overflowing Debt to Balanced Finances: Small Habits Matter

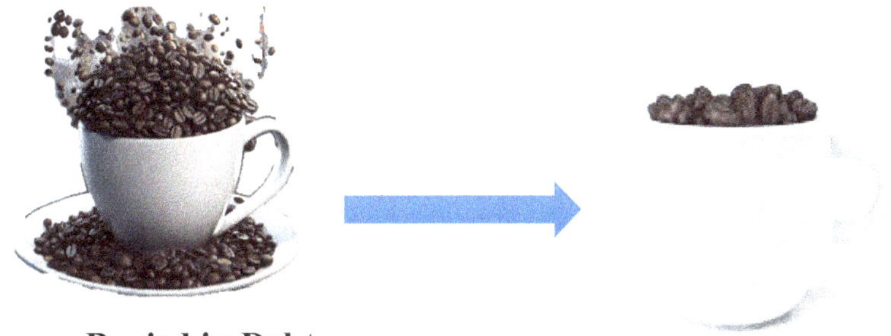

Buried in Debt

This coffee cup overflows with coffee beans. The overflowing beans symbolize an overwhelming financial burden.

Weight of Debt (Heavy Espresso Shot)

- Just as a heavy espresso shot can weigh down your coffee cup, debt can weigh down your financial situation.
- The interest on debt is akin to the heaviness of an espresso shot. It adds to the overall burden and can make it challenging to get ahead financially.

Debt-Free and Thriving

A balanced amount of coffee beans in this cup represents a debt-free financial life. By establishing small, regular financial habits, you can achieve a balanced, debt-free financial life and thrive.

Key Habits

- Create a Budget
- Reduce Unnecessary Expenses
- Pay Bills on Time
- Build an Emergency Fund
- Pay Down Debt Regularly
- Invest for the Future
- Review Your Finances Periodically

Debt can restrict your financial freedom and limit your ability to save, invest, or achieve your financial goals; much like a heavy espresso shot can limit the capacity of your cup. Just as you might dilute a heavy espresso shot with water to make it more manageable, addressing debt often requires a strategic approach, such as paying it down gradually and managing interest.

Successfully reducing and eliminating your debt can provide a sense of relief and financial freedom, lightening the weight that debt imposes; much like lightening the weight of an espresso shot to enjoy a balanced cup of coffee.

DIFFERENT BLENDS OF DEBTS

Much like there are various coffee blends, there are different types of debt, each with its own characteristics. We'll explore the differences between secured and unsecured debt, fixed-rate and variable-rate loans, and how they can affect your financial life.

Debt comes in many forms, much like the various coffee blends. From credit card debt to student loans and mortgages, each has its own flavor, interest rate, and repayment terms. It's essential to understand these differences to tackle your debt effectively.

Credit Card Debt (Espresso Blend)

- Interest Rate: Typically high-interest rates, often exceeding 15%.
- Repayment Options: Minimum monthly payments, but it's advisable to pay the full balance to avoid high interest charges.
- Comparison to Espresso: Like a strong and intense espresso, credit card debt can hit you hard with its high-interest rates, making it essential to address quickly.

Student Loans (Medium Roast)

- Interest Rate: Varies but can be moderate, especially for federal loans. Private loans may have higher rates.
- Repayment Options: Various repayment plans, including income-driven options.
- Comparison to Medium Roast: Student loans offer a moderate flavor of debt. They provide some flexibility in repayment options, similar to the balanced taste of a medium roast.

Mortgage (Dark Roast)

- Interest Rate: Generally lower than credit cards and student loans, often in the single-digit range.
- Repayment Options: Typically long-term (15-30 years) with fixed or adjustable rates.
- Comparison to Dark Roast: Mortgages provide a stable and substantial financial commitment, much like the richness of a dark roast coffee.

Personal Loans (Mocha Blend)

- Interest Rate: Varies based on creditworthiness but can be moderate to high.
- Repayment Options: Fixed monthly payments over a specified term.
- Comparison to Mocha Blend: Personal loans offer a blend of flexibility and interest rates. They can be versatile, much like a mocha blend combines different coffee types.

Auto Loans (Caramel Macchiato)

- Interest Rate: Typically moderate, based on credit history and loan term.
- Repayment Options: Monthly payments with a fixed interest rate.
- Comparison to Caramel Macchiato: Auto loans offer a sweet spot between interest rates, making them similar to the enjoyable taste of a caramel macchiato.

Payday Loans (Instant Coffee)

- Interest Rate: Extremely high, often exceeding 300% on an annual basis.
- Repayment Options: Short-term loans with a lump-sum repayment on the borrower's next payday.
- Comparison to Instant Coffee: Payday loans are like instant coffee; they provide quick access but come with a high cost and aren't suitable for long-term use.

Medical Debt (Decaffeinated Coffee)

- Interest Rate: Varies but often lower than other types of debt, though late fees and penalties may apply.
- Repayment Options: Negotiable payment plans, and some providers offer interest-free options.
- Comparison to Decaffeinated Coffee: Medical debt is less intense, much like decaffeinated coffee, but it's still essential to address it to avoid unnecessary complications.

People have different coffee preferences; carefully consider your financial situation and choose debt types and repayment strategies that align with your needs and goals.

THE CAFFEINE CRASH OF DEBT

The feeling of being weighed down by debt can be just as draining as a caffeine crash after a coffee binge, especially if you have high-interest debt. It's like being stuck in an endless coffee cycle that you can't seem to break free from.

When you compare the experience of a caffeine crash and a financial crash side-by-side, you can see the parallels between the two. This highlights the importance of breaking free from debt and regaining control of your finances.

Caffeine Crash	**Financial Crash**

Caffeine Crash

Symptoms

- Fatigue
- Irritability
- Poor Concentration
- Headaches
- Energy Slump
- Mood Swings

Cause

- Excessive Caffeine Consumption
- Dependency on Caffeine
- Lack of Balance
- Overstimulation

Solution

- Reduce Caffeine Intake
- Establish a Balanced Routine
- Prioritize Quality Sleep
- Stay Hydrated
- Gradual Weaning Off Caffeine

Message

Both excessive caffeine consumption and irresponsible financial choices can lead to undesirable outcomes. In the case of caffeine, it can result in a caffeine crash, while in the case of finances, it can lead to a financial crash. To avoid negative consequences, it is essential to maintain balance, practice moderation, and exercise self-control. Prioritizing your well-being can help you break free from these vicious cycles.

Financial Crash

Symptoms

- Financial Stress
- Anxiety
- Sleepless Nights
- Overwhelming Debt
- Loss of Income

Cause

- Poor Financial Habits
- High Debt Levels
- Unplanned Spending
- Sudden Expenses

Solution

- Budget and Financial Planning
- Emergency Fund
- Debt Repayment Strategies
- Savings and Investment Goals
- Seeking Financial Advice

Message

If you find yourself entangled in reckless financial habits, it's crucial to break free from them and establish healthier habits. You can regain control over your life and finances by planning and seeking guidance. This way, you can pave the way to a brighter future.

Explanation

The representation compares the symptoms, causes, and solutions of both a caffeine crash and a financial crash to highlight their similarities. Just as excessive caffeine consumption can lead to a caffeine crash, poor financial habits and high debt levels can result in a financial crash. The message emphasizes the importance of breaking free from both cycles by establishing healthy habits, planning, and seeking guidance to regain control of one's life and finances for a brighter future.

BREWING A DEBT-REDUCTION PLAN

Now that you're well-versed in the flavors of debt, it's time to create a debt-reduction plan. Similar to a barista who grinds coffee beans to perfection, you will grind away at your debt and watch it diminish over time. Start by making a clear list of your debts, set achievable goals, and develop a strategy for repayment. As you make consistent payments and reduce your debt burden, you'll feel the financial weight lifting off your shoulders.

CHAPTER 5: COFFEE AS AN INVESTMENT

This chapter will explore the exciting concept of treating coffee as an investment. We will discuss how to roast your financial future by selecting the right "beans" (investments) for your portfolio, just as coffee beans are roasted to perfection.

Think of coffee as an investment; each bean represents a financial asset. Similar to how you carefully select beans for their origin and flavor, you can meticulously choose investments that align with your financial goals and risk tolerance. Investing, much like enjoying a fine coffee involves both art and science.

To illustrate how considered investment choices lead to financial growth, let's compare a cup of finely brewed coffee (representing a well-thought-out investment) with an uneven, unbalanced cup (representing hasty investment decisions).

FINELY BREWED COFFEE (WELL-THOUGHT-OUT INVESTMENT)

* Quality Ingredients (High-Quality Beans and Water)

  Just as a finely brewed coffee starts with high-quality beans and water, a well-thought-out investment begins with thorough research and selecting quality assets.

* Balanced Flavor (Diversification)

  A well-brewed coffee offers a balanced flavor, combining different elements for a delightful taste. Similarly, a well-thought-out investment portfolio includes diversification across various asset classes (e.g., stocks, bonds, real estate) for risk mitigation.

* Precision (Strategic Planning)

  Brewing coffee requires precision in measurements and timing. Likewise, a well-thought-out investment plan involves strategic planning, setting clear goals, and considering the timing of investments.

✳ Patience (Long-Term Focus)

Enjoying a cup of finely brewed coffee often requires patience. Similarly, successful investments often require a long-term perspective to allow compounding and growth to take place.

✳ Satisfaction (Financial Growth)

A well-brewed coffee satisfies the palate, and well-thought-out investments can satisfy your financial goals by generating growth, income, or both.

UNEVEN, UNBALANCED CUP (HASTY INVESTMENT DECISIONS)

An uneven, unbalanced coffee may result from inconsistent ingredients. Hasty investment decisions can lead to erratic choices without proper analysis.

✻ Bitter or Weak Flavor (Lack of Diversification)

An uneven coffee might taste bitter or weak due to a lack of balance. Similarly, hasty investments without diversification can lead to uneven returns and higher risk.

✻ Imprecise Preparation (Lack of Planning)

An unbalanced coffee may result from imprecise preparation. Hasty investments often lack thorough planning and can lead to suboptimal outcomes.

✻ Short-Term Focus (Impatience)

Rushed decisions often focus on the short term, like instant coffee. Hasty investments may not allow time for growth to occur and may lead to disappointment.

✻ Discontent (Financial Setbacks)

An unbalanced coffee may leave you dissatisfied, just as hasty investment decisions can result in financial setbacks and dissatisfaction with your outcomes.

Much like a finely brewed coffee offers a balanced, satisfying experience, well-thought-out investments involve quality research, diversification, strategic planning, patience, and, ultimately, financial growth.

In contrast, hasty investment decisions can lead to unbalanced outcomes, emphasizing the importance of careful consideration and a long-term perspective in achieving your financial goals.

SELECTING YOUR INVESTMENT BLEND: DIVERSIFYING YOUR PORTFOLIO

Now, let's explore the diverse world of investments, much like the rich variety of coffee beans. You choose your coffee beans based on flavor and origin, also, carefully select your investments. From stocks and bonds to real estate and retirement accounts, there's a world of options.

Diversification is your financial equivalent of trying different coffee blends – it can be your financial friend, reducing risk and enhancing your portfolio's taste.

DIVERSIFICATION

INVESTING IN DIFFERENT ASSET CLASSES, REGIONS, AND INDUSTRIES

Creating a diversified investment portfolio is like assembling a collection of various coffee cups, each representing different assets. Let's use this analogy to illustrate how diversification leads to a well-balanced financial plan.

DIVERSIFIED INVESTMENT PORTFOLIO: A COLLECTION OF COFFEE CUPS

Stocks (Espresso Cup)

- Espresso cups represent stocks in your portfolio.

- Stocks are like a shot of energy, offering high growth potential but with some ups and downs.

- Just as a mix of espresso cups can give you different flavors, diversifying in various stocks spreads risk.

Bonds (Medium Roast Mug)

- Medium roast mugs symbolize bonds.

- Bonds provide stability, like a balanced coffee flavor. They offer regular income and lower risk compared to stocks.

Real Estate (Café Latte Bowl)

- Café latte bowls represent real estate investments.

- Real estate, like a comforting latte, can provide steady income through rental yields and   potential   for appreciation.

Mutual Funds (Cappuccino Cup)

- Cappuccino cups depict mutual funds.

- Mutual funds combine different ingredients (assets) like a cappuccino's layers, offering diversification in a single investment.

Precious Metals (Mocha Java Cup)

- Mocha Java cups represent investments in precious metals.

- Precious metals, like the unique Mocha Java blend, add diversification and protection against economic volatility.

Savings Accounts (Instant Coffee Packet)

- Instant coffee packets symbolize savings accounts.

- Savings accounts offer safety, like instant coffee's convenience, but typically come with lower returns.

THE BALANCE OF DIVERSIFICATION

Just as a well-balanced coffee collection caters to different tastes and moods, a diversified investment portfolio spreads risk across various asset classes.

- **Risk Reduction:** Diversification lowers the impact of poor performance in one asset by offsetting it with gains in another.

* **Steady Returns:** A diverse portfolio can provide more stable returns over time, similar to enjoying a variety of coffee flavors.

* **Income Streams:** Different assets generate income at various rates, contributing to a steady cash flow.

* **Long-Term Growth:** Like savoring a cup of coffee, patience with a diversified portfolio can lead to long-term financial growth.

* **Adaptability:** Diversification allows your portfolio to adapt to changing market conditions, much like coffee can be enjoyed hot or iced.

Diversification is a way to tailor your investment portfolio to meet your financial goals and risk tolerance, just as you choose different coffee cups for different occasions.

The Take Home Lessons

The key takeaway is that diversifying your investments across various asset classes, much like blending different coffee types to create a balanced flavor, can be an effective strategy for managing risk and achieving financial success. It allows you to enjoy the benefits of different investment options while reducing the potential negative impact of any single asset's performance.

BREWING WEALTH THROUGH CONSISTENCY: THE ART OF REGULAR CONTRIBUTIONS

Now, let's discuss one of the most powerful concepts in personal finance: compounding. Just as coffee flavors intensify over time, your savings can grow exponentially when you invest them wisely. Small, regular contributions to investments can turn into substantial financial growth.

Regular contributions to your investment portfolio are like the consistent pouring of water in a coffee machine. By automating your investments, you'll ensure a steady stream of contributions, much like a coffee drip, resulting in a richer financial blend.

Regular contributions and patience are the secret ingredients to brewing financial success. Let's demonstrate the power of consistent investments over time using a simple example.

Scenario

Imagine two individuals, Alice and Bob, both starts with an initial investment of $1,000.

Alice consistently invests $100 per month into a well-diversified portfolio with an average annual return of 7%.

Bob does not invest regularly and keeps his initial $1,000 in a savings account with a 1% annual interest rate.

Year-by-Year Comparison

Year 1

- Alice invests $100 x 12 months = $1,200.

- Bob's savings account earns 1% interest on $1,000, resulting in $1,010.

- Alice's portfolio grows to $1,000 (initial) + $1,200 (investments) = $2,200.

Year 5

- Alice has invested a total of $100 x 12 months x 5 years = $6,000.

- Assuming a 7% annual return, her portfolio grows to approximately $6,868.56.

- Bob's savings account grows to $1,000 (initial) + ($1,000 x 0.01 x 5) = $1,050.

Year 10

- Alice has invested a total of $100 x 12 months x 10 years = $12,000.

- Her portfolio grows to approximately $15,226.70, thanks to compounding.

- Bob's savings account grows to $1,000 (initial) + ($1,000 x 0.01 x 10) = $1,100.

Year 20

- Alice has invested a total of $100 x 12 months x 20 years = $24,000.

- Her portfolio grows to approximately $41,166.26, showcasing the power of consistent investments and compounding.

- Bob's savings account grows to $1,000 (initial) + ($1,000 x 0.01 x 20) = $1,200.

Key Takeaways

Alice invested $100 every month and her initial investment of $1,000 grew significantly over time due to the compounding effect.

In contrast, Bob did not invest regularly and experienced minimal growth in his savings account balance despite having the same initial amount.

This scenario demonstrates the importance of consistent investments, even with a modest monthly contribution, for substantial wealth accumulation over the long term.

The power of consistent investments lies in its ability to harness the benefits of compounding, which allows your money to grow exponentially over time. Starting early and staying committed to a regular investment strategy can make a significant difference in achieving your financial goals.

CHAPTER 6: BREWING FINANCIAL SUCCESS

We have explored the financial aspects of our beloved Java bean. Just like a skilled barista mixes the right beans, water, and technique to create the perfect cup of coffee, we can blend the lessons from our coffee-inspired financial adventure and offer practical tips for building a secure financial future.

Similar to crafting the perfect cup of coffee, achieving financial success requires a recipe. You have learned that making mindful choices, controlling small expenses, managing debt, and investing wisely are all ingredients in this financial recipe. But how do you put it all together?

BREWING FINANCIAL SUCCESS - A STEP-BY-STEP PLAN

Here's a financial success plan that outlines the key ingredients (choices, expenses, debt management, and investments) and the steps to achieve financial success. By following this financial success plan diligently, you'll brew your own financial success over time.

Ingredients

- ❖ **Choices (Your Financial Blend)**

  - Clear Financial Goals

  - Smart Decision-Making

  - Discipline

  - Financial Education

- ❖ **Expenses (Balancing the Budget)**

  - Essentials Budget

- Savings Budget

- Debt Repayment Plan

❖ **Debt Management (Reducing Financial Weight)**

- Debt Assessment

- Debt Repayment Strategy

- Emergency Fund

❖ **Investments (Growing Your Wealth)**

- Investment Goals

- Diversified Portfolio

- Consistent Contributions

Instructions

❖ **Set Clear Financial Goals**

- Start by defining your short-term and long-term financial goals. What do you want to achieve financially? Be specific and realistic.

❖ **Make Smart Decisions**

•	Use financial education to make informed decisions. Research and understand your options before taking any financial steps.

❖ **Embrace Discipline**

•	Discipline is your financial barista. Stick to your budget, savings plan, and investment strategy consistently.

❖ **Financial Education**

•	Education, like a rich mocha, adds value to your life. Continuously educate yourself about personal finance.

❖ **Create an Essentials Budget**

•	Begin with a essentials budget that covers necessary living expenses like housing, food, transportation, and insurance.

❖ Design a Savings Budget

• Allocate a portion of your income to savings and investments. Treat it as an   essential expense, just like rent or groceries.

❖ Formulate a Debt Repayment Plan

• Assess your debts and create a debt repayment strategy. Prioritize high-interest debts and allocate extra funds toward   them.

❖ Emergency Fund

• Brew up an emergency fund. Just as foam tops a well-brewed coffee, an emergency fund   cushions your finances against unexpected expenses. Aim for at least three to six months' worth of living expenses to handle unexpected financial setbacks.

❖ Set Investment Goals

• Define your investment goals, whether it's retirement, a home purchase, or education. Your goals will guide your investment choices.

❖ Build a Diversified Portfolio

• Create a diversified investment portfolio that includes various asset classes like stocks, bonds, and real estate to spread risk.

❖ Make Consistent Contributions

• Commit to making regular contributions to your investments, regardless of market fluctuations. Consistency is key to long-term growth.

❖ Define Your Retirement Age

• Retirement, like a strong espresso, requires planning. Define your retirement age and the lifestyle you aim to maintain. Calculate how much you need to save for a comfortable retirement.

❖ **Monitor and Adjust**

- Regularly review your financial plan, track your progress, and make adjustments as needed to stay on course.

❖ **Seek Professional Advice**

- Consider consulting a financial advisor to help fine-tune your plan and provide expert guidance.

Key Takeaway

Brewing financial success is a gradual process that takes time, much like brewing a cup of coffee. Achieving your financial goals requires patience, consistency, and a well-structured plan.

CHAPTER 7: SIPPING YOUR FINANCIAL SUCCESS

64

In this final chapter, we will discuss the results of your financial

journey, much like savoring a

fine cup of coffee. We will

explore the wisdom you've

gained along the way, the

importance of continual learning, celebrating small wins, sharing

your financial knowledge, and ensuring a full-bodied financial

future.

Just as a cup of coffee brimming with your favorite brew is a sight

to behold, a well-planned financial future is a sight of pure

satisfaction. Reflect on the knowledge you've gained, for it is the key

to unlocking your financial potential.

The Continual Brew of Learning: Expanding Your Financial Knowledge

Your financial journey is not a one-time event but a continual exploration, much like coffee connoisseurs continuously seek new flavors. Learning about personal finance is an ongoing journey. Stay curious and keep exploring new financial concepts. Read books, follow financial news, and engage with others in the financial community.

Savoring the Small Wins: Celebrating Financial Milestones

Financial success is not just about the grand achievements; it's also about savoring the small wins. Just as a coffee lover appreciates the intricacies of a single-origin brew, you can celebrate your financial milestones, no matter how modest they may seem. Whether it's paying off debt, reaching a savings goal, or achieving a higher level of financial security, acknowledging these milestones fuels motivation and keeps you on the path to success.

Sharing the Wealth: Passing on Financial Wisdom

Like passing on a secret coffee blend recipe, sharing your financial wisdom can benefit others. Consider sharing your financial knowledge and success with others. Teach your loved ones about responsible financial habits and the importance of planning for the future.

A Full-Bodied Financial Future: The Rewards of Your Journey

As we conclude our coffee-inspired financial journey, it's time to appreciate the full-bodied flavor of your financial future. Remember that every choice, every budgeted dollar, and every investment was a step towards a more secure and fulfilling future.

You now possess not only the wisdom to make informed financial choices but also the tools to brew your own financial success story.

May your financial future be as satisfying as your favorite cup of

coffee.

Cheers to a life well-brewed!

ADDITIONAL RESOURCES

Congratulations on completing your journey through the world of personal finance, guided by the delightful aroma of coffee. We hope you've found this book both informative and enjoyable.

To continue your financial education and refine your money management skills, here are some additional resources and tools to explore.

1. Canva Templates:

- Monthly Budget Brewing Planner

- The Latte Factor Expenses Checklist

- Coffee Cup Saving Tracker

- Savings Goal Planner

- Debt Payment Tracker

- Investment Portfolio Tracker

Download link: https://bit.ly/3PRwaMY

As you go through the checklist and mark items that may be unnecessary or excessive in your   life.

- Consider your financial goals and whether these expenses align with them.

- Evaluate the impact of these expenses on your overall budget.

- Identify areas where you can cut back or find more cost-effective alternatives.

- Redirect the money saved toward your savings, investments, or other financial priorities.

The latte factor expenses checklist will help you to identify areas where you can reduce spending and make more mindful choices with your money.

2.   Excel Worksheets:

- Annuity investment Calculator

- Balance Sheet

- Expenses Calculator

- Financial Independence, Retire Early (Fire) Estimator

- Financial Vision

- Loan Amortization Schedule

- Net Worth

- Personal Budget

- Retirement Planner

Download link: https://bit.ly/3FmzrPQ

71

72